Repentance—
THE JOY-
FILLED LIFE

Repentance— THE JOY-FILLED LIFE

M. Basilea Schlink

BETHANY HOUSE PUBLISHERS
MINNEAPOLIS, MINNESOTA 55438
A Division of Bethany Fellowship, Inc.

The author of this book may be contacted at the following address:

Canaan in the Desert
9849 North 40th Street
Phoenix, Arizona 85028

Library of Congress Cataloging in Publication Data

Schlink, Basilea.
    Repentance—the joy-filled life.

    Translation of: Busse—gluckseliges Leben.
    1. Repentance. I. Title.
BT800.S3513 1984   234'.5   83-23774
ISBN 0-87123-592-7

M. BASILEA SCHLINK is the founder and director of the Evangelical Sisterhood of Mary in Darmstadt, Germany, and Phoenix, Arizona. She is the author of many books and holds a Ph.D. in Philosophy and Psychology from the University of Hamburg.

Other books by the same author:

Behold His Love
Father of Comfort
Hidden in His Hands
I Found the Key to the Heart of God,
     autobiography
Mirror of Conscience, booklet
My All for Him
Praying Our Way Through Life, booklet
Realities of Faith
Ruled by the Spirit
Those Who Love Him
You Will Never Be the Same

Foreword by the Sisters of Mary
for the Eighteenth American Edition

"Repent, for the kingdom of heaven is at hand" is written in large letters at the entrance to the little Land of Canaan, in West Germany. Repentance is the treasure that our founders, Mother Basilea and Mother Martyria, discovered many years ago — the secret of a joy-filled life, for he who is forgiven much loves much, as we read in the Gospels. And this renewal spread. Repentance is like a stone thrown into water, producing concentric circles of ripples.

A spiritual movement has arisen, a "kingdom of heaven" movement you could say. Many all over the world, including large numbers of young people, have begun a new way of life. They have experienced the redeeming power of Jesus testified to in this bestseller:

"It was a busy winter evening and I was hurriedly fixing dinner when the phone rang...a voice I had not heard for a long time was on the other end: 'Could you come over? We need help,' he said...I arrived at their home...it was a home of beauty, luxury, and cars in the driveway, beautiful children, seemingly a prosperous, happy home. I found only distress, packed suitcases (hers), tears, bitterness and despair. The decision was already made to separate from each other. We talked briefly...getting nowhere. I asked her if she would take a ride with me alone for a cup of coffee, just to talk...We returned to my house and I went in to get a little book...called 'Repentance' by Basilea Schlink and I asked her if she would only promise me one thing, that she would read this book carefully and submit to the Lord Jesus! Then if she still wanted to leave her husband, then go, there was nothing else I could do. This has been three years ago and they are still living together. 'Repentance' is an interstate highway to the Father's heart and His love and forgiveness..."

"It has been life changing to read the book called 'Repentance'. My heart longs for deeper repentance as never before. The prayer at the end of the book has been my cry to God each day...I had settled into a comfortable, compromising type life style. I really loved Jesus but I was settling for much less than I really could have. I wasn't serious enough about following God's commandments either...Repentance is taking on a new meaning and I am discovering the joy that results from doing it...There's something new being born in my heart. A deep cry for God's highest..."

"While reading 'Repentance...' tears coming from

nowhere started flowing from my eyes and I found myself prostrate on the ground repenting and confessing my sins. Fears that filled my life went. The people whom I used to find difficult in our church and others, I found myself loving them genuinely..."

"For the past two weeks I felt as if the corners of my mouth had been permanently tied down so I couldn't laugh or smile and I wondered why. Jesus has shown me that I had a few loose ends in my life and some very deep repenting to do. I am so thankful for what He has done because I can smile now and I feel it inside and out...It will be one book I will read over and over..."

"I am a prisoner in a county jail, but a free man in Christ Jesus...I enjoyed reading your book on 'Repentance — The Joy-filled Life'. I do testify indeed to this grace of our Lord Jesus. He sanctifies us, heals and releases rivers of living waters from inner depths. 'Repentance' has given me a life of victory..."

It is our prayer that many others throughout the world will come to experience the secret of a joy-filled life as they read this book. May that which has helped us so much now help and bless them too.

Darmstadt, West Germany   *Spring 1984*

Contents

Chapter 1

A Confession

Everything that is written in these pages is part of the confession of my own spiritual experiences. My Christian life began with contrition and repentance, but it was not until some years later that I discovered how precious daily repentance is. A letter to my friend and co-worker written in the year 1936 tells how this came about. It was her birthday, and the Scripture text on the calendar for that day read, "Who is a God like thee, pardoning iniquity?" (Micah 7:18). I wrote to her: "We can praise and glorify God for many things, but no exultation on earth can or will surpass the exultation over God's gift of the forgiveness of sins. The song of rejoicing, 'Bless the Lord, O my soul', resounds not only here on earth, but throughout the heavenly spheres, for there is joy in heaven over one sinner who repents. And

18

if the anthems of praise for all God's goodness to us in this life cease one day, another song will be raised by the heavenly throng above — the song of the Lamb who has borne our sins.

"Does this song of thanksgiving resound in our hearts — 'Who is a God like thee, pardoning iniquity' — or do our prayers lack this note of praise? If so, how can we then join in singing the song of the Lamb at the throne?

"At the beginning of last year, we scarcely knew the song of jubilation expressed in this verse of Scripture. But do you remember when we first found Christ? You will recall your confirmation classes and the time in Kassel, and I my time at Bible college. Among my favourite songs then were, 'O the joy of being redeemed...' and 'There is a fount where holy blood for wretched sinners flows...When I was sunk in sin and woe, for me the blood of Jesus flowed, so I'll rejoice until I die and praise the crimson tide...'

"Yet all those years, while I was studying and waiting and you were engaged in social work, our hearts were so laden with the things of this world, so insensitive and complacent that the song of the Lamb died away, and our hearts no longer knew this exultation, 'Who is a God like thee, pardoning iniquity!' We had resigned ourselves to the fact that we were not victorious over certain sinful traits in our characters. We were no longer so grieved about these bonds as we were before — and consequently we no longer had a daily encounter with the Redeemer and could no longer rejoice over His forgiveness and His power to deliver us from our sins. We strayed farther and farther along this path, without realizing that it was leading us away from Christ.

"But God in His grace sought us, so that our hearts could once again sing the song of praise to the Lamb and so that we could be with Him on His great day. By the grace of God we became strongly aware of our sin and bondage in the past year — during our work in winter but especially last summer with X. One thing we both learnt was that we cannot forgive, be merciful, suffer injustice or react with meekness. In our present state we shall not be able to take our place with the overcomers one day, for without sanctification no one will see the Lord. O to think that God gave us an awareness of our sin this past year! What could have been greater!

"What other verse could we have received for your birthday than this verse of thanksgiving, 'Who is a God like thee, pardoning iniquity'? What could have been more fitting, especially in view of the lost years?

"Now we can begin our ministry. Previously, we weren't really able to do so, for unless one's heart is filled with this song of jubilation, one can't pass on the good news of the forgiveness of sin. One can only do so and have the power and authorization to carry out such a ministry if one's heart rejoices, 'His blood has washed all my sins away,' and if with shining eyes one points to the Lamb — the Lamb who has accomplished the greatest and most wonderful deed. Is this not a wonderful verse for this year? Seldom have we had such a verse. It does not only show us our sins, as we saw them during the past year, but this word of God is also a promise — a promise that this joyful shout, 'Who is a God like thee, pardoning iniquity!' will resound in our hearts. With joy we shall be able to testify to this gracious and merciful God who forgives us all our sins in

Christ and who sets us free from the law of sin and death. And then this will bring a blessing to our ministry.

"The old year brought us the knowledge of our specific bonds and the forgiveness of God. The new year, let us solemnly resolve, will be devoted to fervent struggles and wrestling in prayer, so that we may overcome our sins, for, 'if the Son makes you free, you will be free indeed.' We want to remain steadfast and resolutely battle in prayer for the victory. We want to thank God for all the obstacles that He has placed in our way. Oh, that we would learn to leap over them by continually showing love! Oh, that we would learn to overcome our sins! It is pure grace that God does not only reveal our sins to us, but also gives us an opportunity to learn how to be victorious in all the difficulties and to overcome bit by bit. Let us use every aid in the Word of God and every other weapon that He has given us that will help us to be victorious in this difficult situation with X. After being forgiven, we want to attain His victory no matter what it might cost. With thanksgiving we want to praise His victory and testify to how God has helped us."

In the previous years I no longer cried over my sins. That is why my prayers no longer knew the joyous shout, "Who is a God like thee...", as I wrote. I could not bear a joyful witness to this God. And the joy of heaven, which should be our portion in Jesus, was missing in my life. For the same reason my love for Jesus had become so lukewarm. Only penitent sinners, who are granted forgiveness, are set on fire with love for Jesus. So I can testify how impoverished a life without daily repentance is. Heaven does not draw near. The radiance of joy is missing. There is no adoration or songs of praise. Love for Jesus is not burning in one's heart. There is no power in one's ministry, and it bears no fruit.

I can never thank God enough for showing me that this was the cause of the problems in my spiritual life and the reason why I could not gain the victory in my battle against sin. This was the root of my spiritual death. And God, who answers prayer, answered my prayer for a repentant heart. The Lord answered in very specific ways. He allowed my relationship to those with whom I was living to be utterly shipwrecked. He showed me that I was unable to love truly those who were hard for me to bear. In this way He convicted me of my sins and gave me a contrite heart.

As I had the privilege of tasting the renewed life and joy that came from contrition and repentance, it became my earnest prayer to receive this precious gift daily. Soon my co-worker and I began to pray that the youth groups we were leading would also experience the blessing of repentance, leading to new spiritual life. God answered by working in their hearts through the teaching of His Word. Later when we experienced His judgment in the bombing of our city in September 1944, contrition and repentance broke out in the youth groups and dead hearts became spiritually alive. And now those who experienced this time can testify with us to the blessings of contrition and repentance. In the months following the destruction of our city everyone was filled with fear and terror. We were under continuous attack from the low-flying aircraft. The German army was disbanded. The allied forces entered the city.

But we experienced that heaven was close to us, especially when we had a retreat with the young people for several days while the battles raged on. Yes, it is really true. The girls' faces were radiant with joy; adoration and love for Jesus had filled their hearts and made them so happy that the perils of war vanished before the reality of heaven, which had come down. The words of Jesus had come true, "Repent, for the kingdom of heaven is at hand."

In the Sisterhood of Mary, which was born out of this experience, we later had similar experiences. Time and again in His fatherly leadings God had to discipline us. He was waiting for us to respond with contrition and repentance, so that heaven could come down to us and He could give Himself anew to us. How long He often had to wait for this response! But in His mercy the Spirit of God does not allow us peace till He has again brought us to contrition and repentance. The times of "fellowship in the light" that we regularly hold in our community also serve to this end; on these occasions we help each other to see ourselves and our sins in the light of God. But then God lets us experience ever anew how life and joy break forth from contrition and repentance – rejoicing and songs of praise, which not only permeate our evening meetings when we worship together, but our entire life.

Praise and adoration be to God, the Holy Spirit, who awakens in hard, dead hearts the grace of contrition and repentance. He gives it to those who ask for it, and in this way He brings heaven down to us.

Chapter 2

Repentance — A Creative, Life-Giving Power, Bringing Joy

Long ago John the Baptist cried out, "Repent, for the kingdom of heaven is at hand." Is that not the very basis of the Gospel, the Good News? Repentance — the gateway to heaven! Repentance — the gateway to the very heart of the Father! Repentance makes us joyful, for it brings us home to the Father, home to heaven. It is a gift of the Holy Spirit, who inclines Himself to a human heart, which is hard and self-assured. He breaks it into small pieces, so that the Father, the Creator, can take these pieces into His hand and mould a new vessel to His glory.

Should we not ask for this gift more than all others? It brings divine life, true life. Hearts that can cry and rejoice are alive. Only a dead person is incapable of giving any reaction. He is rigid and lifeless. He can no longer move. He cannot express his joy and he is unable to weep. However, a person who lives in contrition and repentance has the characteristics of life. He weeps over the one thing that is worth weeping over, since it spells death and terrible judgment for us and all mankind and will have horrible consequences here and in eternity if there is no repentance. Yes, he weeps over sin. Deeply sorrowed by sin, he no longer weeps over things that are not worth weeping over, for compared with this sorrow, they are only a trifle, transient matter. Whoever gets too upset about temporal things and weeps over them too much falls into a sadness that leads to death (2 Corinthians 7:10). But whoever weeps in repentance over that which is truly lamentable, over that which will have such great and terrible consequences, weeps aright.

Thus the penitent are actually sincere, truthful and realistic. They sorrow for their sins before it is too late, unlike others who neglect to do so and will be sorry for their sins for all eternity. They are grieved over their sins now, so that they can turn over a new leaf and begin to lead a new and different life.

Yes, those who repent are truly alive, for after weeping over their sins, they break out in a rejoicing and singing that is unknown to other hearts. The joy of forgiveness — no other joy can compare in depth and height! The joy of redemption that far surpasses all other happiness. A person who has been imprisoned in chains for many years rejoices when he is released. And yet his imprisonment was only for a limited number of years — and his freedom too is limited by time. However, here we are speaking of release from bondage to the prince of this world, the prince of the kingdom of hell, a captivity that would have lasted for eternity and from which no human being could have effected release. And now such a release *has* been effected. Our Lord came down from heaven, took on human flesh, let Himself be taken prisoner, bound and condemned to death in our stead, so that we could go free. Shouldn't that make a human heart rejoice as never before? Again, it is only contrition and repentance that let us partake of this joy, this renewed life. By making us conscious of our sinful bondage and spiritual death, they drive us into the arms of our Redeemer and life-giving Lord.

Therefore, people who have not experienced repentance, even though they may be devout and faithful churchgoers, are spiritually dead, as our Lord Jesus says in the letter to the church at Sardis: "You have the name of being alive, and you are dead" (Revelation 3:1). To be spiritually alive is to live in repentance. Spiritually dead are those Christians who never weep over their sins or who have long ceased to do so. Dead — in God's eyes — are those Christians who can no longer rejoice over God's forgiveness. Whenever this joy is missing, even if we may call ourselves committed Christians, there is something wrong in our lives. For just as it is true that we sin ever anew and need forgiveness ever anew, it is also true that repentance should pour into our hearts ever anew. Yes, contrition and repentance should become the very basis of our life. Otherwise, our entire Christian life is on a downward path, and we shall become like the "proudly exultant ones", who Zephaniah says will fall under severe judgment (Zephaniah 3:11).

Furthermore, repentance should be the foundation of our life, because this is the only proper attitude that we can have towards God. Can we come before God, the holy God, in any other way than as contrite sinners? We can only lie at His feet, because we are sinners, who daily sin against Him. Moreover, repentance should be the foundation of our life, because we daily sin against our fellow men. Truly, there is no one among us who lives in perfect love. When we think of those with whom we share our home or with whom we work, should we not also lie at their feet with contrite hearts? Perhaps they make life difficult for us, but we become guilty if we do not bear them in love and help them to set their lives straight.

"Repent!" — that is the call of Scripture. Time and again we hear this call from Jesus Himself. And it was the message that Martin Luther proclaimed, for he said that the life of the Christian should be daily repentance. He fought against lifeless and false religiosity, against the self-assurance and pride with which we dare to approach God and which causes the divine life in us to stagnate. Do we realize how much our Lord Jesus wants us to live in this penitent attitude, so that we might have life? If this were not so important to Him, the impenitent attitude of the church at Laodicea would not have caused Him to pronounce such a severe verdict: "You say, I am rich, I have prospered, and I need nothing; not knowing that you are wretched, pitiable, poor, blind and naked. So, because you are lukewarm, and neither cold nor hot, I will spew you out of my mouth." (Revelation 3:17 & 16).

Are not these words valid today also? If we think that everything is all right in our life or in our church or fellowship, if we insist that we are right and have done everything we should have done in our relationships with those who cause us trouble, then we have an attitude of self-assurance, which is the opposite of repentance. Then we assert that Life, that is, Jesus Himself, who would come to us with His forgiveness, has no room in our heart. To the complacent and self-assured Jesus says in His letters to the seven churches, "Repent!" Yes, He appeals to us to turn from this attitude, which brings ruin to believers. Only those who overcome will not be blotted out from the book of life one day (Revelation 3:2-5). Only repentance can save us from spiritual death and lead us to eternal life, and only repentance lets us have a foretaste of this divine life here and now.

Only those who are alive can bring life to others. The spiritually dead are unable to generate life, because there is no life in them. They cannot be a testimony to others by their deeds. They are simply dead. Whoever does not live in repentance belongs to the spiritually dead, who cannot bring anyone to life. But the penitent are full of life, divine life; and they can bring others to life. Whenever someone repents, he scarcely needs to say a word. He doesn't need to preach at others. Rather, when he lies prostrate before God and man and confesses with a broken and contrite heart, "I have sinned; I am guilty," his words have the power of life. They can open the hardest hearts and bring to life the spiritually dead. These words, spoken by the prodigal son, as he lay weeping before his father, caused the father's heart to overflow with love. The same thing happens whenever we confess our sin and admit our guilt before our fellow men. When we ask them for forgiveness, their hearts are opened. Tears of contrition soften even the hardest hearts, even though some cases may take longer than others. Contrition and repentance transform us and others. They give birth to love and new life.

What a creative, life-giving power is inherent in repentance! For that reason our Lord Jesus calls the seven churches in Revelation to repent. For the same reason the Apostle Peter proclaimed the call to repentance at Pentecost. Repentance is the way to new life. It brings us the Holy Spirit. With repentance the kingdom of heaven is at hand.

Chapter 3

Repentance Brings the Kingdom of Heaven Down to Earth

"Repent, for the kingdom of heaven is at hand." Isn't that what we are all longing for? Don't we all wish to have a foretaste of heaven and see the kingdom of heaven take shape in our midst? The kingdom of heaven! That means peace and joy. That means that love reigns. That means that there is true happiness, because Jesus is really in our midst.

But where can we find a church or a Christian organization that depicts the kingdom of heaven? The people who work together would have to live in love and complete unity. The spirit of adoration would have to be alive. Joy would have to shine on all the faces. Yes, places that radiate heaven would attract people, even those who no longer want to have anything to do with the Church. Everyone would like to experience a foretaste of heaven on this poor earth, for everyone, even the most irreligious person, hungers for joy, love and peace. Everyone hungers for a foretaste of heaven. The word "heaven" strikes a note in everyone's heart, for all men are Adam's children, driven out of paradise, but still cherishing a deep desire for the lost paradise. When they find the kingdom of heaven, a ray of paradise here on earth, they are attracted to it. This would be the best place for them to learn to believe in Jesus, who is the Lord of the kingdom of heaven and who alone represents the very nature of heaven: peace, love and joy — everything that man longs for.

How distressing that we Christians in our churches, Christian organizations, brotherhoods and sisterhoods do not depict the kingdom of heaven, even though our Lord Jesus said that He brought the kingdom of heaven to us! How sad it is that our sermons about the love and glory of Jesus convince so few people, because our lives do not reflect the kingdom of heaven! They find no place where they can experience the kingdom of heaven and taste how good the Lord is. Jesus, however, came to build the kingdom of heaven. At the start of His ministry He said that the kingdom of heaven was dawning. Now He is waiting for it to be established among us. He suffered bitter death on the cross not only that we might go to heaven one day, but that His redemption might be demonstrated in our lives here and now. And whenever His redemption is manifested, there is a foretaste of heaven, for the redeemed depict it as people in whom love, peace and joy, reconciliation, kindness and meekness reign.

Yes, God is waiting for the manifestation of the kingdom of heaven among us Christians. And the world is yearning to see it. If God says, "The kingdom of heaven is at hand," should we not be able to see it somewhere? In the Person of Jesus it drew near to us and was offered to us. He came to us to bring heaven down to earth. For wherever Jesus, the Lord of heaven, appeared, there was a foretaste of heaven on earth. Those who were with Jesus tasted it. They tasted the Father's love, the goodness and kindness and loving care of their God. They tasted the forgiveness of the Father, a love that healed all the wounds of the soul. They tasted the joy that is given to sinners who come to their Saviour. Yes, abundant joy filled the hearts of those who had the privilege of beholding Jesus and hearing gracious words from His lips as He drew close to them in His love.

But when the Head, Jesus Christ, ascended to heaven, His Body remained here on earth. And this Body should in turn bring heaven to men, so that they would become whole in body and soul when they come into contact with its members. They should rejoice, be comforted and be healed of their wounds. They should be loved with kind, merciful, forgiving, forbearing love whenever they come together with members of His Body, and in being loved they should experience a foretaste of heaven.

"The kingdom of heaven is at hand," said Jesus when He came to earth. Now He is also saying this of His own. However, we ask ourselves once more, "Where is it at hand?" Can we say, "Go to this or that house or church and there you will become a cheerful person, healed of the sorrows of your soul. You will be surrounded with so much love that you will feel like a new person. You will taste the fullness of joy in this fellowship, because the presence of eternal joy can be sensed there"? Is not the opposite true of our churches? That is why there is no attraction for those who do not know Jesus. No wonder that large numbers of people prefer to go to the forests and parks on Sundays to seek joy. There in the midst of creation they experience the cheerfulness and beauty that nature reflects. There they find a bit of the joy that every human heart longs for. When they go to church, they often do not sense any joy, they do not see it on the faces. They do not find the radiance of God there as they do out in nature. In what church or fellowship can they sense that hearts are really singing along in the worship services and meetings, so that their hearts are also swept along to joy in the Lord Jesus Christ?

Where are the childlike and trusting believers who reveal the truth of Jesus' saying that the kingdom of heaven belongs to those who become like little children, so that others can taste heaven in their midst (see Matthew 18:3)? Yes, where are the childlike believers who have the power to attract unbelievers, who then in the light of this childlike joy become joyful? To a great extent our Christian lives are governed by our intellect. We are so stiff, so unchildlike and therefore so joyless. It grieves the heart of God that we Christians are so lacking in joy, childlikeness and friendliness that we reflect less of the kingdom of heaven than His creation does. As a result we make Christianity unattractive for those who do not know Him.

Do we have any idea how much God suffers because of what we continually do to Him? Or, expressed in human words – which Holy Scripture uses time and again to show us the heart of God – how often God is disappointed in us! He is especially disappointed by the Christians who do not reflect His image, although He has ransomed them with the precious blood of His Son so that they could be a witness to Him and bring others to Him. What a grief this must be for God! The very stones, indeed all of nature will preach, because we, the members of His Body, keep silent, because we do not radiate the joy of redemption and are such poor witnesses for Him.

Now comes the great question. Why is there so little of the kingdom of God, the kingdom of heaven, in our midst that the world cannot be renewed, people cannot be attracted, souls and bodies cannot find true relief, the sad cannot be comforted? Why? There is one word that ushers in the kingdom of God: "Repent!" It is a call as mighty as a peal of thunder. It is so loud and clear that it cannot be ignored. It is a call to us human beings, for we are all sinners. Yes, it is not simply *a* call; it is *the* call of Scripture. Whoever does not heed this call will neither gain heaven nor any other gift or blessing from God — not even forgiveness. It is a holy law of Scripture that God with His blessings only draws near to a humble soul, to a sinner that repents. It is only to such souls that the kingdom of heaven draws near. It remains closed to all others. For the kingdom of God, the kingdom of heaven, is the kingdom of grace, and grace is only given to those who lie at the feet of Jesus as penitent sinners.

That is why the first characteristic of the kingdom of heaven is the overflowing joy that comes from contrition and repentance. Repentance is the gateway through which the Gospel can come to us. Repentance is the gateway to a joy-filled life with Christ, for it is the prerequisite for attaining forgiveness, and wherever forgiveness is received, there is salvation and joy. Contrition and repentance bring abundant happiness, for they contain the joy of being pardoned when one deserves to be condemned now and in eternity. Contrition and repentance bring us the joy of being accepted again as a child of God, for He says, "Your sins are forgiven." Yes, repentance brings us the bliss of heaven. When a repentant son returns home, the Father not only takes him in His arms, but He also clothes this contrite child with the robe of righteousness, puts on him a ring of love and the most beautiful jewels, and these same jewels will one day adorn him in heaven. The penitent are the rich. They are bestowed with gifts and pardon, because they are the poorest of the poor who no longer have the right to claim anything from God or man. Because they have "squandered" everything, because they have become guilty, they lie as miserable sinners before God and man, waiting to be looked upon with favour, waiting for a gift, the word of forgiveness to be pronounced over them.

What could bring more joy than a word of pardon spoken to a condemned man? It makes him sing and dance with joy! Yes, the kingdom of heaven, the kingdom where everyone rejoices and sings, only dawns in a heart that has received forgiveness.

Moreover, the kingdom of heaven is the kingdom of love. But we can only love if He loves us first, and God loves the contrite of heart, the penitent sinner. Jesus did not come to the righteous, but to the sinners. He bestows His gift of forgiveness on those who come to Him, the Saviour, in contrition and repentance. In His love He tasted death for them and pronounced forgiveness on the cross. In His love He will set them back on the right path, and they will become whole. Sinners with broken and contrite hearts have but one desire. Filled with thanksgiving, they want to love Him who loved them so much. They are so overwhelmed that He has borne their sins and carried them away. When we receive forgiveness, our hearts are so filled with joy that we cannot help but love Him with a lavish love. We cannot help but give our lives to Him who gave His life for us and set us free from the prison of sin. We cannot stop thanking Him, and so we do everything possible to bring Him joy and to bestow our gifts upon Him, serving Him with all our talents and strength. And this is what heaven is all about: centring upon Jesus and loving Him above all else.

Repentance truly lets us experience the kingdom of heaven with all its blessings, for it brings us the most beautiful and most wonderful gift: an overflowing love for Jesus. For is it not the greatest longing of a Christian to love Jesus? How many people have said wistfully, "If only I could love Jesus with all my heart!" They sense that then their lives would have meaning and fulfilment. Then they would be the person that Jesus wants them to be, able to respond to His love. Their lives would be enriched, because whoever loves is rich. Then they would be truly happy.

What a joyful message! Repentance is the way that leads us to this lavish, wholehearted love for Jesus, bringing with it such a great treasure of grace and blessing. We see this in the life of Mary Magdalene. She had nothing to bring Jesus but her sin, for what had she done to God and man! Yet her life was so enriched by the deep love that repentance kindled in her. She became an example for us all. Indeed, repentance is the gateway to the kingdom of love, the kingdom of heaven. There is no other way for us to enter the kingdom of heaven or for it to come to us; no other way for us to experience it here on earth.

Yet is it not true that everyone who professes Jesus Christ as Saviour has at one time knelt down at the foot of the cross as a penitent sinner, received forgiveness, and in this way entered the kingdom of God? Why then is there so little evidence of the kingdom of heaven in their churches and fellowships? As long as we are on earth and not in heaven, it is a spiritual law that no one obtains a permanent right to the kingdom of God through his conversion or baptism. How many times does Scripture teach us with admonitions and illustrations that one can lose the grace that one has received, the very next moment like the unmerciful servant (Matthew 18:23-35) — if one does not forgive his brother, if one harbours bitterness in his heart or is unmerciful! But are we not all liable to this time and again? Therefore, there is only one way to come under the grace of God again and to open the door for the kingdom of heaven and that is to come with our sins to God immediately — and when necessary to others — in contrition and repentance.

If we repent ever anew, Jesus will be drawn to us ever anew and dwell in our midst, bringing with Him the kingdom of heaven, which is always present where He is. The thief on the cross accepted his punishment, confessing, "We are receiving the due reward of our deeds" (Luke 23:41). He asked Jesus for mercy and Jesus responded by promising that he would be with Him in paradise. The same applies to us. If we come to Jesus

ever anew like the thief on the cross, we shall experience paradise on earth with Him, for the kingdom of
heaven is at hand whenever sinners repent.

Chapter 4

Repentance — God's Appeal to the Christians for the Sake of Their Nation and Its Well-being

"Repent!" — who hears this call? It is as though Jesus is passing through the nations and the Christian churches today, knocking at the hearts of individuals and calling with a loud voice, waiting for someone to hear. This call is meant first for the family of God and not the world, since judgment will begin with the household of God (1 Peter 4:17). But the question is, "Do we even realize it when God chastens and judges us?" If we did, we would respond by repenting, by repenting ever anew and turning from our sinful ways. For when God judges, He is waiting for a response; He is waiting for our repentance. It is not a matter of waiting only for un-believers to repent, as a result of evangelizations, for instance — although we should also make this a real concern of prayer. No, today it is of vital importance that the family of God repent.

Surely we have a great need for repentance as members of the Body of Christ, for even in our personal lives we have time and again hardened our hearts against the Spirit of God. Jesus' last request was that we be one, but we have responded with division, hatred and severe criticism of each other. And although there has been an improvement in the relationship between the major branches of Christianity, how much condemnation, criticism, strife, quarrelling and disputing do we still tolerate between our various Christian denominations? We do not treat each other as brothers in Christ and we still set up walls of doctrine, although the Enemy and all his hordes have already set out for the final battle, and the most varied groups on the anti-Christian front are banding together! In our day inner unity is essential if we are to be strong and withstand the attacks of the Enemy. And the only way to attain oneness of love — which was Jesus' fervent prayer for His own, so that they would be a testimony to the world — is by contrition and repentance. The tragedy of division will never be ended unless every one of us in his own fellowship and denomination begins to repent personally by opening his heart to the criticism he receives from other Christians with different views.

In other words, we are lacking repentance — repentance for the blatant, serious sin marring our lives as believers: the division within the Body of Christ. Repentance would also sweep away our unloving attitude, which is a characteristic of spiritual death, for repentance invariably gives birth to new life. Wherever there is repentance, there is happiness and life, according to Martin Luther. Thus in our times our main need does not lie in better or more modern sermons, organizational set-ups and ecumenical conventions but in repentance, this God-given gift to weep over our lack of love, our faultfinding and criticism of each other. Repentance has become rare; it is scarcely to be found anywhere. At evangelizations people who were far away from God have come in from the street, repented, turned from their old ways and given their lives to Jesus. But do we who attend churches and fellowship meetings know that our lives should consist of daily repentance, daily coming home to Jesus, daily kneeling down at the foot of the cross and bringing Him our sins, above all the sin of disunity? When we as members of one Body, whose Head is Jesus Christ, contend with each other and are envious of each other, we sin against Jesus Himself.

This sin weighs heavily upon the Body of Christ and will call down the judgment of God. In Germany there is an even greater sin weighing upon us Christians and that is the crime our nation has committed against Israel, God's chosen people. Six million Jews were killed; because of this the wrath of God is upon us. As Christians we are especially to blame. For when the terrible crime occurred and millions of Jews were tortured with inhuman cruelty and killed at the hands of German people, the Church in our country remained silent. The Christians did not stand up as the Danes did and protest the injustice. With the exception of a number of individuals the church members were not driven by the desire to help the Jews at all costs. Nor did they ring the church bells the night the synagogues were burnt down.

The Church gave no reaction — an indication that she was dead. Because we were silent, we heaped guilt upon ourselves, and we were struck by the judgment that later descended upon our nation. Our churches were destroyed. Germans were killed by the thousands in the bombings. Refugees thronged the streets, and the Iron Curtain divided our country.

We have sinned, but where is repentance in the Church? The Lord expects her to see what she did, to confront the fact that our nation, of which we are members, has sinned against the very apple of God's eye and that unlike the Good Samaritan we passed by him who "fell among robbers" and did not act like disciples of Jesus.

It took years before the Christians of our country gradually came to recognize this sin. Yes, it took us a long time before the first flicker of repentance began to glow in us and before we had a new attitude toward Israel, God's chosen people, an attitude of love. And yet all the attempts to show repentance and make amends are but a grain of sand in comparison to the immense sin that weighs upon us. To this very day voices can be heard in our land objecting, "We didn't have anything to do with this. It was Adolf Hitler; it was the S.S. We weren't involved; we can't take the blame for this!"

As the Church of Jesus Christ we must realistically face up to the sins that can be found in our ranks — division and other sins against love, unwillingness to repent of the crime committed against Israel, hardness of heart and a pharisaical self-assurance. But above and beyond this the Church is inflicting the greatest suffering of all upon God when in her ranks the living God is declared dead. All of us are indirectly involved in this, because the lives we live often seem to declare that God is dead.

When the "death-of-God" theology is heralded throughout the world today, we must realize that it is not a purely intellectual matter. God is not being declared dead because modern man cannot fit Him into his conception of the world, but because the human race, including us Christians, are "dead in sin". This is why people today are declaring, "God is dead". By our everyday actions, by our unwillingness to admit our mistakes and sins, we Christians have declared God dead — perhaps without even realizing it. For if we no longer want to humble ourselves before God and man, acknowledging our sins, if we no longer want to repent, we do not need a living Saviour. Then in the end we are no longer able to form a concept of the living God, whose very nature is holiness.

To a large extent God's commandments, the holy proclamation of His will, are also declared "dead" today in the Church, that is, they are declared invalid — on pseudo-theological grounds. With this the declaration of God's death has been sealed. We have conformed to the spirit of our times instead of taking a stand against the evil watchwords of our times, which demand that laws, commandments, ethics must change and conform to the concepts and needs of modern man. Do any of us repent because of all these blasphemies directed at God by the very members of His Body?

The spirit of contrition and repentance has by and large become foreign to us. Repentance implies returning to God. Instead of repenting, however, we demand that God adjust to our modern concepts. Because the spirit of contrition and repentance is missing, church services, evangelizations and other Christian meetings often lack power and cannot move the listeners to tears of contrition. How very much we, the members of the Body of Christ, have hardened our hearts! We no longer want to see sin for what it is. When God is dishonoured and blasphemed and His commandments are abandoned, we do not regard it as such. Nor do we see that when God Himself is declared dead in His Church and His commandments are no longer regarded as binding, these are the signs of the times that Jesus said we should watch for. Nor do we see that by going along with the crowd or apathetically tolerating the rebellion that has broken out against God and His commandments, we are actually furthering the advance of the powers of darkness in the end times.

The increasing lawlessness and the fact that love has grown cold — signs that Jesus specifically named for the end times (Matthew 24:12) — are put aside by the Church as being of no great importance, although the unprecedented facts and examples are alarming. We need but call to mind certain trends in the past years. The soaring crime rate. The glorification of brutality and perverse forms of sex. The increase in drugs, which have already claimed millions of addicts. The alarming growth of involvement in occult activities, in spiritism and even satanic cults.*

And all this is taking place in "Christian" nations, yes, mainly in these countries, and even in their churches. Who takes this as a challenge to pray, fast and repent? Nineveh, a pagan city, was prophesied destruction if it did not repent. But the people did repent, and this repentance saved them. How much more so should there be repentance today in Christian circles, fasting and prayer, so that a terrible judgment would not descend upon us for our great iniquity!

---

* For examples of this development see M. Basilea
  Schlink's booklets on current topics.

Today the words of Joel are applicable: "Blow the trumpet…sanctify a fast; call a solemn assembly" (Joel 2:15). Out of love for Jesus, who is filled with compassion when He sees mankind on the brink of destruction, and out of love for our fellow-beings let us "snatch them out of the fire" (cf. Jude v. 23). In this case a traditional type of prayer will not suffice. It is essential to pray with fervent entreaties and tears, "Lord, spare Your people and do not deliver them up to their shame. Do not let Your New Testament people continue to honour false gods and deny and dishonour You, so that the nations and non-Christians sneer, 'Where is your God now?'" Long ago the servants of the Lord and the people repented; they began to weep and pray. And God's answer was, "Then the Lord's love burned with zeal for his land, and he was moved with compassion for his people" (Joel 2:18 NEB). Let us not keep God waiting in vain for our entreaties and prayers. Today too God wants to act according to His word, "Amend your ways and your doings, and obey the voice of the Lord your God, and the Lord will repent of the evil which he has pronounced against you" (Jeremiah 26:13).

Thus one thing is essential: that we as Christians finally hear the call to repentance, because it contains grace for us as individuals and also as a body and as a nation. "Awake, O sleeper," Jesus Christ is calling to us today (see Ephesians 5:14). Self-assurance spells death! The fact that we were once spiritually alive will not help us if we are spiritually dead today and are not living in a spirit of repentance for our personal sins and the sins of our nation. God instructed the Prophet Ezekiel to proclaim, "When a righteous man turns away from his righteousness and commits iniquity...none of the righteous deeds which he has done shall be remembered; for the treachery of which he is guilty and the sin he has committed, he shall die" (Ezekiel 18:24). If we were once in a good spiritual condition, but now no longer, it is the present condition that counts with God, not the previous one. The very existence of our nation depends upon whether we repent of the times we have incurred guilt; if not, God will requite us for our deeds. Our eternal fate depends upon whether we repent personally, for only those who are of a humble and contrite heart will inherit the kingdom of God. For this reason it is vital not only for our church, but also for every individual member in the Body of Christ, that one and all live in the spirit of repentance and have a contrite heart.

Our spiritual effectiveness in the Body of Christ and in our nation depends upon whether we have a deep contrition and repentance for our sin and our nation's sin and whether we lie in contrition at the feet of those who have suffered from our sin and whether we long to perform acts of love for them with a penitent heart. In the power that comes from repentance His own will be light and salt for the world. If we have true contrition and repentance, we long to make amends for what we have done wrong, we long to do good and show love to those whom we have grieved or harmed. We read that according to God's commandments when someone had sinned he had to bring a guilt offering and if he had stolen something, he not only had to pay it back, but was also required to add a fifth to it (Leviticus 5:16). If this was expected under the Old Covenant, how much more then must the principle apply to us as people of the New

Covenant when we make amends in contrition and repentance for what we have done wrong! The love that Jesus has won for us by His sacrificial death longs to make amends and do good without measure, as He bids us in the Sermon on the Mount.

People who are genuinely sorry for their sins are grateful for every opportunity to do an act of kindness for those whom they have wronged. How much good would be done in our churches and in our nation if we lived in contrition and repentance! How many amends would be made that are pleasing to Jesus! Wounds and breaches would be healed, and in the end we would see that by the grace of God many a good thing has come from our sins and failures. If true contrition and repentance seeks and loves punishment, as Luther says, how much more will it seek to make amends! A penitent heart will seek to do all that lies within its power. Thus there is nothing that brings about so many good fruits in our life as a contrite, penitent heart.

And so repentance is the sole foundation upon which everything in the kingdom of God is to be built. Then our spiritual "house" will have a firm foundation and it will not be swept away when a storm comes. All our service in the kingdom of God that is not built upon contrition and repentance will not be of eternal duration. It will not bring true fruit. O that repentance would once more be a gift we would covet for ourselves personally and for our churches! It contains the greatest blessing and grace for us all.

Chapter 5

The Way to Repentance

Since repentance brings great joy and new life, nothing is more important than finding the way to repentance. The first step is to realize the fact that we do not have repentance. This is fundamental, for since the fall of man there is nothing we lack more than this one thing. It is the lament of all the prophets. It is God's lament over His people. John the Baptist lamented over this and finally Jesus Himself lamented, saying, "Would that even today you knew the things that make for peace..." (Luke 19:42). We are apathetic and indifferent towards our sins, and we are usually not disturbed by them at all. We are more likely to weep over what is done to us, or over difficult leadings. We weep over our sorrows, troubles and disappointments. Each one of us does so, for this is our human nature. But not everyone comes to the point of true contrition and repentance and weeps over his sins. Such reactions are foreign to human nature. The human heart has a way of thinking it is always in the right and has no need to weep over its sins. By nature we are self-confident and impenitent. We blame others or even accuse God when we do not understand His ways.

Having taken the first step and realized that we do not have repentance, we shall come to a second realization, namely that we cannot bring ourselves to repentance. No one is capable of changing his own hard heart into a soft, contrite heart that is able to weep over its sins. It is a gift of grace from heaven when this is accomplished in us, for we are totally unable to do so.

However, once we have realized that we are lacking repentance and that we cannot bring it about ourselves, it is essential that we do not get stuck here but look in faith to the omnipotent God. For we have a God who performs miracles, and that is our comfort. God wants to perform miracles. He says, "Is anything too hard for the Lord?" (Genesis 18:14). It is a joy for Him to create something in our hearts that is not there by nature, and He does so through the working of the Holy Spirit. To the glory of His name He is able to perform such miraculous works and melt even the hardest of hearts.

Our Lord Jesus Christ came to break our hard-heartedness and self-righteousness and to make our hearts humble and soft, so that we can weep over our sin. When Jesus destroyed Satan's power, He also destroyed the hardness of our hearts and the blindness towards our sin, which the Enemy has used to ensnare us. Jesus also destroyed our impenitence and won for us the ability to weep over our sins. Thus there is hope for us to become penitent, not only weeping over our own sorrows, but weeping genuine tears of repentance for the suffering that our sin has brought to God and to our fellow men. Thus, Jesus' call, "Repent!", is also a promise, for He does not require anything without giving us the power to fulfil it. And when He sacrificed His life for us at Calvary, Jesus put to nought all the principalities and powers that could hinder us from coming to repentance.

If we are discouraged because we lack repentance and excuse ourselves by saying that it does not lie in our power to obtain a contrite heart, because repentance can only be granted as a miracle of the Holy Spirit, it is a sign that our thinking has been clouded by the Enemy. And because our human nature always seeks an excuse, we finally blame God if His gifts of contrition and repentance are not to be found in our lives.

But we really have no excuse when we do not have repentance. Jesus won it for us on the cross, and God has shown us that we can obtain it by the prayer of faith, trusting in the victory of Jesus. It is precisely when we become aware of the hardness of our hearts and our complete inability to repent by virtue of our own strength that we should pray all the more earnestly for this gift. Jesus said, "Whatever you ask in my name, I will do it." And since the prayer for contrition and repentance is a prayer in His name, we have the assurance that He will answer it. Jesus has come to redeem us from our impenitence and self-righteousness. He has come, that we might become penitent sinners, who return home to the Father like the prodigal son. Whoever comes to God with this prayer, trusting in His help, will not be disappointed.

This prayer is certain to be answered. If we daily pray, "Lord, give me the grace of repentance. Grant me a broken heart and a contrite spirit. Help me to see the 'log' in my own eye (Matthew 7:3) and to recognize how I have sinned against God and man", He will answer our prayers. He will open our eyes to see the depths of our sin, so that we shall be grieved by that which we have done to God and our fellow men. Then suddenly instead of weeping over what others have done to us, we shall weep over that which we have done to them. We shall be able to see everything in the light of truth and no longer in the murky light of the Enemy, who magnifies the other person's sin and covers up our own sins, so that we either do not see them at all or only see them as a small speck.

The prayer for the light of God, the light of truth, to be shed into our lives, upon our words and deeds is an important prayer, for our sight is veiled in darkness, especially when we take a look at ourselves. The Enemy is eager to keep us in the dark and prevent us from seeing our sin, because he does not want us to repent and be filled with divine life, joy and power. However, since Jesus has come, we no longer need to be under the power of the Enemy. For Jesus has said, "I am the light of the world; he who follows me will not walk in darkness, but will have the light of life." His light of truth will shine upon our pathway, that we may see when we go astray.

Yet it is not enough to pray daily that the Lord would give us the light of truth. It is not enough to ask Him daily to give us repentance. No, if we want repentance, we need to submit willingly to the chastening hand of the Lord day by day. Only if we pray daily, "Father, do with me whatever You will. Chasten me, so that Your chastening hand will break me and give me a humbled, contrite heart," will contrition and repentance be given to us. Probably more people have come to contrition and repentance through the chastenings of God than through sermons on the need for repentance. Thus whoever longs for the grace of repentance should not only pray for this blessing, but also be willing to accept every chastening, so that his heart can be made soft and broken and there can be room for repentance. Repentance does not fall from heaven like a shower of blessings. After praying for it and claiming it in faith, we shall receive it as a gift during what can be hard chastenings and sufferings. But it is worth committing ourselves to follow such pathways, and those who do not evade them are blessed, for the most wonderful fruit will come from them.

It is almost incomprehensible how much new, divine life is born out of contrition and repentance. All true joy, all power and authority in our ministry for the kingdom of God depends upon whether we live in the blessed state of repentance, weeping over our sins and humbling ourselves before God and man as we admit our guilt. Therefore, let us give everything for this one gift of grace. Let us not cease to pray and beseech the Lord to grant us repentance, being willing to accept chastenings. But let us also confront the main obstacles keeping us from coming to repentance.

O Holy Ghost, please give to me
A penitent humility,
The greatest of Your graces.
For all my sins You will impart
Abundant sorrow to my heart,
To make me truly humble.

O Holy Ghost, please make me see
My lukewarm heart's complacency
And bring me to repentance.
Help me for all my sins to mourn,
Which for my sake my Lord has borne
In such great pain and suffering.

Come, Holy Ghost, I pray, to me,
That You my Advocate may be
And plead my wordless longing.
You see, as hard as stone, my heart;
Tears of contrition now impart.
O grant me true repentance.

Spirit of penitence, I pray,
Give me a new, pure heart today,
A broken heart, most humble,
That I, before both God and man,
Humbly acknowledge my great sin,
Which grieved my Lord so deeply.

Jesus, my Saviour, I believe
This contrite spirit You will give,
For in Your Word it's promised.
Jesus, I know You will impart
A truly contrite, lowly heart.
You are the sinner's Saviour.

Chapter 6

The Main Obstacles in Coming to Repentance

Part 1: *No repentance, because we are self-righteous, proud and unwilling*

The chief obstacle to repentance is our self-righteousness. We know it is really a miracle when a pious person weeps many tears of contrition and lives in a penitent attitude, because it is precisely for the "pious" that the danger of self-righteousness is so great. Thus it is essential that our self-righteousness be dethroned and broken to pieces, so that Jesus can come to us as the Saviour of sinners, whether it be to an individual, to a church or to a fellowship.

Self-justification — that is, claiming one's innocence and thus in the final analysis blaming God — is an inheritance we have received from Adam and Eve. Even

the worst criminals have this urge to exonerate themselves. They claim innocence in the face of the most
heinous crimes. Prison chaplains write that there is no
place like a prison to find so many self-righteous
people, maintaining that they are actually innocent.
They think they have been imprisoned unjustly. We
human beings have an excuse for everything and thus
we see no reason why we should repent and turn from
our ways. If we think we are in the right, that we have
good reason to justify ourselves and say that we are not
guilty, why should we repent?

If we defend ourselves, become vehement or aggres-
sive or angry, we excuse ourselves by saying that it is
perfectly all right for us to react like this, because we
were not shown respect or were not treated properly.
We think we cannot let others treat us like a doormat all
our lives, and so we have to defend ourselves. No matter how angry, vehement or abusive we are, it is the
fault of the other person who had irritated us and
treated us unjustly. How can we help it if we don't have
nerves like steel? How can we help it if we get upset so
easily, because we are at the end of our strength? Even
if someone falls into the sin of adultery, it was something he never really wanted to do. He was just unable
to control himself when too greatly aroused. Is it his
fault that God created him with such strong desires?
How can he be blamed his whole life long for something
that he actually did not want to do? How unfair for his
whole life to be ruined just because of one weak moment!

Or perhaps our marriage was agony for us. We were
misunderstood by our spouse. And then God sent
someone into our life who seemed to be created just for

us. We were a perfect harmony of heart and soul. Could it be a sin to become attached to this person? We didn't even go that far! Or we are bitter, filled with envy and hatred if God did not give us talents, if we are often a wallflower, if we do not succeed in life, because we are not so gifted or intelligent, if we cannot win people with beauty and charm. If this is the case, how can we possibly react differently?

We can go on thinking in this way without realizing that we are actually putting the blame on the Lord and preventing Him from drawing near as the Saviour and the Source of joy, and from filling our lives with His joy, peace and radiance. We accuse Him for giving us bad dispositions, unstable nerves, so few talents. We blame Him for placing such severe penalties on anger, bitterness (Matthew 5:22; Galatians 5:20f.), on small lies, adultery, and so on. We argue that we have to help ourselves when we are in trouble, and that our strong human drives got the better of us. And so in the long run Jesus is always given the blame. Today it is no different from long ago. Jesus is accused by us all, and we are innocent, even if our sins and wicked deeds may have destroyed the lives of others. By making excuses and trying to explain how it all happened, saying that we had no other choice but to speak or act in a certain way, we have become blind. We can no longer see that sin is sin, that guilt is guilt and that we are responsible for our failings.

How self-righteous our hearts are we can tell by listening to statements that are made even in circles of committed Christians. Because we do not want to be at fault, we blame God and say that He is responsible for wars and all the other misery in the world. People say,

"How can God let that happen? How can God remain silent about all the wicked things that happen on earth, about all the terrible crimes that are committed?" And here again self-righteousness makes us blind and deaf. We no longer perceive how God speaks in judgment through wars and all the other troubles in the world. Yes, He is speaking powerfully. Such judgments are His last attempt to win us back in love. People no longer perceive how those who come to God in the midst of judgment, willing to listen to His voice, humbling themselves beneath His hand, expecting comfort and help from Him alone, are comforted abundantly by Him. Indeed, by His presence He transforms hell into heaven on earth — even in prison camps. On the other hand, the self-righteous are so blind that they do not see that it is we human beings alone who are to blame for all the misery in the world, because we do not want to obey God. If we obeyed God, living according to His commandments, He would not have to chasten and judge us. There would be heaven on earth.

By our self-righteousness we grieve His heart today as His accusers did during His Passion. If we always find ourselves, our country or the world innocent, we place the blame on God, who is the very essence of love, and on Jesus who died for our sins and is truly a Saviour, a Helper and the Source of all joy. But He only helps those who seek His help and come to Him as the sick and needy and sinful.

However, because Jesus in His boundless love desires to bring us help, He urges us to repent. Today to His New Testament people His call to repentance is just as emphatic as it was long ago to His Old Testament people. When He calls us to repentance, it is unmistakably clear that we are sinners, we are guilty. For only sinners need to repent and change their ways. If we honestly face this call, it will convict us of our sins. "Repent" means to search our hearts and see where we are at fault. It means to change our minds and attitudes. So change your mind and attitude if you have wronged your brother by withholding forgiveness from him, by not esteeming him better than yourself, by not treating him respectfully, by not loving him with a love that bears all things, suffers all things. Change your mind and attitude if you have sinned against the ninth commandment and have said unfavourable or detrimental things about someone or passed on negative remarks perhaps without even knowing whether they are true. Change your mind and attitude if you have conformed to the world and no longer taken the truth seriously. Change your mind and attitude if you are no longer following the path of Jesus, the path of the cross and sacrifice. Yes, change your mind and attitude — this is the meaning of the word "repent" in the letter to the church at Laodicea. This is the trumpet call that the Lord is sounding to His New Testament people who are often ruled by self-righteousness and lukewarmness, who tend to lapse into legalism, setting their minds at rest by a mere formal fulfilment of the law, or who live from cheap grace and self-justification.

But Jesus "declares war" on all self-justification. He pronounces judgment on it, indeed the most severe judgment. This is the judgment that He pronounces upon all who are self-righteous, like the Pharisees of His time. Yes, although they were so well acquainted with the Word of God and seemed to take it so seriously, being zealous for the true teaching, praying so much, they were under the Lord's condemnation. The kingdom of heaven was closed to them. True, they too were offered God's grace when Jesus came as the Saviour. But they excluded themselves, because they did not accept the preaching of repentance and were not willing to let go of their self-righteousness. While the people humbled themselves in contrition upon hearing John the Baptist's sermon, the Pharisees refused to follow the call to repentance. They rejected his preaching, found it exaggerated. Perhaps they said, as many do today, it is unhealthy soul-searching, psychological introspection. But God says something different. Our salvation depends upon whether we accept this call to repentance. The gates of heaven will not be opened to us one day if we merely know who Jesus is. They will only be opened to us if we ever anew lie at the foot of His cross as a truly penitent sinner with a contrite heart.

Our objections — whether they be theological or psychological — usually have but one root: It is pride that makes us reject the message of repentance. For repentance means humbling ourselves before God and man, changing our ways and making amends. In doing so, we admit that our former ways were wrong, and that is humbling. No other sin is so firmly ingrained in our hearts as pride, especially in the hearts of those who acknowledge Jesus as their Saviour. If we are told that we are too slow or that we are too fast and impetuous, immediately our pride rebels. We are quick to defend ourselves. We say we work so slowly, because we are thorough. We are so hasty and in a rush, because we are so busy. Or because we must tell someone something emphatically, this is why we are so vehement. How quick we are to reject what others tell us! How fast we are to cast the blame on others, saying they always criticize us and find fault with us, they are not satisfied with anything we do, they do not understand us. But if we cannot accept anything others tell us, we are proud. The humble want to hear what others tell them. They have the courage to hear the truth about themselves and to admit that they need to change. Whether it is a small matter or a big matter, they say, "Yes, it is true. I need to turn over a new leaf."

Jesus calls this attitude of excusing ourselves "seeing the log in our brother's eye and the speck in our own", for when we make excuses for ourselves, we minimize our own guilt and accuse others of blaming us unjustly. Man, in his pride, constantly excuses himself. Since he does not come to contrition, he does not change his ways. Then the sin that he refuses to admit will block him from coming to Jesus. It is not sin as such, but rather unacknowledged and unrepented sin that separates us from God and will cause us to come under judgment in the next world.

O that we would listen to the voice of those who reprove us — whether in major or minor matters — as the voice of God calling us to repentance! How else should we hear His voice than through His instruments who are placed beside us, who see our behaviour, know us and admonish us? If we do not hear the voice of God in the admonitions of those who seek to correct us, but instead reject their help, we shall know few tears of contrition and we shall not have a life of daily repentance. And yet it should be a matter of course for us to repent daily, for in the prayer of confession at church we acknowledge that we are sinners and that we sin daily.

This means that we daily need to repent and daily need to change our ways. If we are lacking repentance, our Christian life is full of hypocrisy and something very important is wrong.

If we hold to the teaching that we are sinners to our last moment, daily contrition and repentance are an intrinsic part of it. But daily repentance is not to be understood legalistically. Some days we are more convicted of sin and there is more repentance in our hearts. On other days when the Lord grants us the special presence of His love, and joy in Him arising out of forgiveness, repentance is more on the sub-conscious level. But in general our lives should speak of an ever new experience of contrition and repentance.

To sum up, as Christians we should primarily repent of our self-assurance and self-justification. Let us begin in our everyday lives to admit our faults when others reproach us or when our conscience quietly admonishes us to admit our failings instead of trying to forcefully silence it with all sorts of excuses. Yes, we must become enemies of all self-pity and self-justification, for as our Lord Jesus said time and again in the Gospels, self-justification will lead us straight to hell. Let us begin to repent of every excuse we utter and even the slightest self-righteous thought. Let us turn from these thoughts and change our ways. Because our Lord accomplished His act of redemption on the cross to set us free from the spirit of self-righteousness, He will hear our prayers and lead us more and more into a state of contrition and broken-heartedness. Then the kingdom of heaven will be open to us and our hearts will be filled with joy, life and love.

Part 2: *No repentance, because we do not recognize
the voice of God calling us to repentance
in His chastenings*

Why is it so hard for us Christians to find the way to repentance? In addition to our self-righteousness there is
another special reason. We are no longer accustomed
to seeing all the events of our life, especially our troubles, in conjunction with the will of God and we do not
realize that He is trying to speak to us through them.
Because we no longer regard Him as the living God, we
find it hard to believe that He has counted the very hairs
on our head and that nothing — not even the smallest
incidents in our lives — can happen without His will.
This is foreign to our way of thinking.

And yet it is true, as Holy Scripture says, that when
God chastens us, when He intervenes in our lives
through troubles and suffering, He is doing so in order
that we may partake of His holiness (Hebrews 12:10).
That is, when He chastens us by leading us into suffering, it is a corrective measure, a purifying process.
There is something in our lives that is displeasing to
Him, and suffering is the chastening hand of God. It is
His loving plan for us, because He is seeking to set us
back on the right path. And He speaks to us by showing
us what should be changed in our lives. It is for this

reason that He leads us into loneliness, taking from us people that we may have become over-attached to. Perhaps their love meant too much to us. However this may be, the Lord desires that our love be centred on Him. Or He may let us become sick, so that we would at last draw closer to Him and see our life in the light of His countenance and come to repentance. Or He may have given us an illness to teach us patience.

Whether the suffering He sends is intended as a punishment or more as a purifying process, the Lord always desires to work in our sinful nature. With loving concern, as a true father, He seeks to bring us up properly, so that we shall be transformed into His image — a process that will last all our lives. In Romans 8 the Apostle Paul says that we have been called and redeemed by Jesus, so that we may be transformed into the likeness of the Son of God.

This is why Jesus came to earth. For this purpose alone did He suffer death for us. He wants us to partake of the divine nature and to reflect again the nobleness of God's image. And for this reason when He chastens us He can ask us to respond by truthfully acknowledging that we do not yet bear God's image. If we ask Him, He will show us where we fall short. He is waiting for us to repent in sorrow that as children of God we reflect His image so poorly and cause Him and our fellow men so much distress.

O that we would take to heart how much the Lord yearns to find the response of contrition and repentance in our lives! When we have repentance, He can work in us quickly and change us bit by bit into the image of Jesus. When we have repentance, His purifying process in our souls will be effective and His chastening will serve to our sanctification, as Scripture says (Hebrews 12:10). However, if we resist Him and do not come to repentance when He leads us along paths of suffering, but instead accuse Him for leading us along such difficult paths, then we deprive ourselves of the blessing of being transformed into His image in suffering and thus we miss out on abundant grace. For God does not punish us for His pleasure (see Lamentations 3:33), but only to achieve His purpose in us. How difficult we make it for Him when we resist Him, when we do not want to humble ourselves in such situations, but say, "What did I do to deserve this?" It is usually so, that when the Lord sends suffering into our lives, we feel as though we are martyrs, that we should be pitied, because we have so much to suffer, because we have so many problems and troubles. This is especially true when we have to suffer because of others. Then we become depressed and dejected and feel that we are innocent and are suffering unjustly. We do not want to humble ourselves beneath this suffering. Yes, when others cause us suffering and make life difficult for us, our hearts are often filled with bitterness and we feel sorry for ourselves. We fall deeper and deeper into self-pity and an imagined state of martyrdom, growing more and more gloomy, discontented and unhappy.

Thus we become imprisoned by our problems. The same is true when God leads us into greater troubles, along hard paths of suffering and chastening. We do not understand the true purpose of God behind it all. And even if we do not accuse Him, the best we Christians often do is to say, "It is God's will" and so finally accept it. But even the Moslems say, "Allah wills it", although they do not know that God is a Father who disciplines

His children. He only chastens and punishes us, because He is waiting for us to feel sorry for what we have done wrong, just as an earthly father would punish his child to make him realize how much he has grieved his father or his brothers and sisters. The father wants his child to change his ways.

One of the great problems for us Christians is that we are no longer accustomed to seeing the hand of God, working in our personal lives through chastenings, because we seldom think of God as our Father. We have lost the ability to hear God's voice in the chastenings, and we do not realize that He is waiting for us to repent. For this reason we often fail to come to repentance in our daily lives, although God seeks to bring us to this place through His chastenings. We only repent if we commit an extremely bad sin. But as Christians we seldom commit such sins, or at least we think so. Little do we realize that the most prevalent sin among believers − criticism, finding fault with others, feeling superior to them − is a flagrant sin in God's eyes. Although He pronounces a severe judgment upon this sin, we do not take it seriously at all. We do not feel any need to repent. And so chastening is meant to help us take our sins seriously before the holiness of God − especially those sins that we consider insignificant.

Holy Scripture teaches that there is a connection between our sin and the chastening we receive. Time and again we perceive this note in Scripture, for instance, in the Wisdom of Solomon, "Wherewithal a man sinneth, by the same also shall he be punished" (11:16 AV). This is a law of God, proceeding from His holiness, but also from His fatherly heart.

In our Sisterhood we have often experienced how

things that happened to us — especially during the time when we were building our Mother House and Chapel with our own hands — were clearly related to our guilt. Sometimes we would experience it in the small things of everyday life. During the construction period the Sisters had to push a dump cart heavily loaded with sand. It was very hard to steer. They were always afraid that it would jump the tracks, for the Sisters scarcely had the strength to get it back on again. One day it jumped the tracks six times. Could it be an accident when we consider that not even a sparrow falls from the roof unless it is the will of God? Should not every happening have something to tell us? Should not every problem — and that really was a problem for our workday life — be a sign that God is speaking to us? God is alive. He is a Father, who cares about all things. He wants to speak to us through everything. The Sister in charge called the Sisters into the prayer tent. Together they came before the countenance of God and asked the Lord to show them whether they had grieved Him and what was the cause of their problem. They asked Him to show them why their work had been in vain. The Sisters then began to confess that on this very morning they had been criticizing each other in their hearts. This prevented God's blessing from being upon their work. The Sisters then repented and were reconciled with each other. They forgave each other wholeheartedly and went back to work. And the dump cart no longer jumped the tracks!

Though it seems to deal with just small problems in everyday life, this story is important, for our life often consists of such small things, and we should learn to see how God is chastening us through them to call us to repentance. I can remember other incidents that happened while we were constructing our buildings. At first we did not want to see the relationship between the things that happened and the hand of the living God. For instance, there was a long period of torrential rain that hindered the work on the house. When it seemed as though the rain would never stop, we finally realized the relationship between God's actions and our sin and we obeyed His call to repentance. Then we experienced His grace. It was the same when God gave us severe frost or heat waves, which hindered progress on the building.

We as modern men often put ourselves above the Word of God. We act as though we were intellectually superior to God. We are too proud to see the hand of God in every event, great or small. Yet Scripture shows us that God thinks differently. There is a relationship between weather and God's dealings with men, as we read, for instance, in Leviticus 26:4, Deuteronomy 11:14; 28:12 and 1 Kings 17:1. Amos 4:7 clearly shows that God uses weather to speak personally with individuals: "And I also withheld the rain from you when there were yet three months to the harvest; I would send rain upon one city, and send no rain upon another city; one field would be rained upon, and the field on which it did not rain withered."

If God takes such trouble with us, setting heaven and earth in motion to bring us to contrition and repentance, should we not ask Him to open our blind eyes and make us willing to hear His voice? O that we would use all the events of our lives, and especially the sorrowful ones, to attain the grace of repentance and to give God the response that He is longing to receive! How precious to Him is one tear of contrition! Truly, it is worth more to Him than a hundred "good deeds". When a soul is filled with contrition and repentance and lies at the feet of God with a broken and contrite heart, there is joy in heaven. And if the angels are filled with joy over such souls, how much more must the heart of Jesus rejoice! And the Father will come to them and take them in His arms. He can perform His great deeds with them, because His glory can shine out through their nothingness. He reveals Himself through the humble and contrite souls and not through the proud who constantly find fault with others and feel superior to them, not even realizing their own sins.

Our repentance will not only bring joy to God's heart when the purpose of His chastening has been attained, but it will also bring joy to us. Then the suffering will no longer crush us; instead it will contain great joy. Then we shall receive help in the midst of suffering. We may even be spared some paths of chastening if we immediately listen to His voice, and then we shall be able to be led along paths of suffering that are not only necessary for the sake of our sin. In this way we shall be able to suffer as priests for others, "that they also may obtain salvation" (2 Timothy 2:10), as the Apostle Paul writes.

But even when we suffer as priests — time and again Scripture speaks of such suffering — we can do so only if repentance is the motivating force. We can suffer for others and for their sins only in the awareness of our own sins and guilt. Only Jesus has suffered innocently. He alone is the sacrifice for our sin. We can only suffer with Him as members of His Body and pray that when we fall into the ground as grains of wheat in suffering, it

may bring forth fruit. And He has died for us sinners, so
that we too can now lay down our lives for our brothers
(1 John 3:16).

Part 3: *No repentance, because we do not take the*
Word of God as binding for our lives

Self-assurance, pride and unwillingness to humble ourselves in contrition beneath the chastenings of God are
obstacles to repentance. But there is another point in
our lives that is decisive, for it determines whether the
way to repentance is open or blocked off. It is the question, "Which standards do we use to measure our
lives?" If we are content with the standard of going to
church, saying our prayers and keeping the Lord's day,
not killing or stealing, then it will, of course, be difficult
for us to come to repentance. If this is our standard,
then our Lord Jesus says to us, "I tell you, unless your
righteousness exceeds that of the scribes and Pharisees
[they kept the Ten Commandments and seemed to be
leading good, pious lives], you will never enter the
kingdom of heaven" (Matthew 5:20).

In other words, our Lord Jesus has a different standard. He tells us that whoever is angry with his brother
will fall under judgment. He requires that we be reconciled with our brother before we leave our gift at the
altar. This does not only apply if we have wronged our
brother, but even if we hear that he has something
against us, if there is something between us and our
brother.

Jesus gives us a high standard, the standard of loving

our enemies. Who can measure up to this? Probably most of us have someone at home or at work or in the neighbourhood that makes life difficult for us, treating us unjustly or perhaps even tormenting us. How do we react? Do we respond with a merciful love for our enemies? Or do we think and say bitter, critical things about those who wrong us? Do we assert our rights? Jesus says that this is sin and He tells us that we shall come under judgment. And His words are true. For when He says, "Till heaven and earth pass away, not an iota, not a dot, will pass from the law" (Matthew 5:18), these words will likewise apply to keeping the rules Jesus gave us in the Sermon on the Mount, which is the law of love, the law of the kingdom of God.

In other words, if we use the Word of God as the standard to measure our actions instead of our own standard, we shall always see our faults and easily come to contrition and repentance. If we realize that we are a sinner, having become guilty towards our brother – or towards our enemy – by not showing him love, by not winning him over with merciful, humble, forbearing love, then it will be easy for us to come to repentance. But if we do not have this standard, we shall not find the way to repentance. Contrition and repentance in turn give birth to new life. Our love for Jesus grows, and we shall love Him with a lavish love. We shall also love our fellow men, even those who are hostile towards us, for we cannot love Jesus without loving our brothers. A warm, overflowing love will be kindled towards everyone once we sincerely repent of our cold, apathetic hearts and for not bearing the weak and difficult in love. If we measure ourselves against the Word of God, our eyes will be opened.

Our repentance should begin with the fact that we have no longer taken the Word of God seriously and have not come to repentance. We dared to use our own standards and were satisfied when we lived up to them. We are like the Pharisees. Outwardly we participate in Christian activities, perhaps even very enthusiastically. We pray, we go to church and Bible studies. We give our offerings or even tithe. We have made a break with the world, refraining from doing certain things. And we think this is enough. We use our own yardstick. But God will measure our lives according to His standards, and we shall have no excuse when we appear before His judgment seat, for He has clearly proclaimed His standards in His Word.

In other words, the reason for impenitence – in our personal lives or in our churches and fellowship groups – is often that we do not measure our lives by the standards set forth in the Word of God. We do not take seriously His standards, for instance, "Give, and it will be given to you; good measure, pressed down, shaken together, running over" (Luke 6:38) or "go with him two miles" (Matthew 5:41). We do not regard them as binding for our lives. As Christians we act the same way that we would in the world, keeping our own interest in mind. Instead of giving to the kingdom of God and the Lord's ministry and to those in need, we set aside as much as possible for ourselves.

Therefore, Jesus' strong words about disregarding Scripture apply to us indeed. We do whatever we want with His Word. We change the meaning till it suits us and can be made to conform with our uncleansed lives. We wish to do as we please in our relationship to our neighbour, with our money and with everything else.

Since we do not apply the yardstick of Scripture to our lives, we are seldom upset about what we do or fail to do, about our prayer life, our unloving relationship to our neighbour and about our faultfinding and gossiping.

Thus we need to repent for having so little repentance. We need to repent of our pharisaical spirit. John the Baptist said to the Pharisees, "Who said that you could escape the coming wrath of God?" (Matthew 3:7 LB). Indeed, we think that if we believe in Jesus, we can escape divine judgment. Just as the Pharisees said, "We have Abraham as our father," we say, "We go to church. We are at home there. We live from grace, and so we shall escape the wrath to come." We must repent of such thoughts and words, for they shall bring us judgment. It was this attitude that caused John the Baptist to call the Pharisees "you brood of vipers" and say to them, "Bear fruit that befits repentance" (Matthew 3:8).

Fruits of repentance, a change of mind and attitude — this is what God is waiting for. Otherwise the axe will be laid to our root, because "every tree...that does not bear good fruit is cut down and thrown into the fire." Whose life shows forth much of the fruits of the Spirit — love, joy, peace, patience — as we read in Galatians 5:22? Is the light of joy shining on our faces? Do we bring joy to others? Are our lives a witness to peace? Or are they filled with quarrels and disputes? Galatians 5:20 tells us that enmity, strife and dissensions belong to the fruits of the flesh and will come under the judgment of God. Who can testify to the fruit of patience — even in many illnesses or in living with difficult people? Who can claim the fruit of kindness, always seeing the good in others and loving them with a love that covers a multitude of sins instead of finding fault with others and talking about them? Who can witness to the fruit of gentleness, having a humble, gentle spirit instead of being vehement, angry and fighting for his rights? Who can say that he is always friendly?

The Apostle Paul writes in his letter to the Galatians (5:23) that there is no law that can bring a charge against the fruits of the Spirit. But the Lord brings a charge against us if He does not see them. As Scripture says with reference to the fruits of the flesh, "Those who do such things shall not inherit the kingdom of God." This is not said to the people of the Old Testament, but to the people of the New Testament, who believe in Jesus Christ. Yes, of what avail is faith if it does not bear fruit? This is why it is so important that we have the right standard, and we find it in the Word of God. The first step is to heed the command, "Repent!" if we are not living in repentance. For repentance should be fundamental to our very way of life.

Chapter 7

God Is Waiting for Us to Come Back to Him in Repentance and to Love Him

Repent! Truly, we should not only repent of our trespasses against the commandments of God in the Sermon on the Mount, but we should repent of the chief sin, the sin against God Himself. According to Scripture this will incur the most severe punishment of God. We insult and grieve the heart of God if we break the first commandment, the commandment to love God above all else. How it grieves Him if we do not love Him, if we ignore Him or only love Him with a divided heart.

God is a Father of love. He has lovingly planned everything for His children: sunshine, the songs of the birds, trees, flowers and meadows, mountains and lakes, the beauty of heaven and earth, and like every earthly father He is waiting for a response from His children. He wants them to rejoice, to thank Him and to give Him much love. But our Father, who created us and who loves us with an unfathomable love, waits in vain. When is He given thanks and praise for all His goodness?

Truly, the birds sing their songs of praise; the flowers blossom to bring Him joy. Yet we human beings, created by Him, usually remain silent, and even those who have become children of God through Jesus still bring Him so very little praise and adoration. Otherwise our faces would shine with joy when we think of all His favours and kindnesses, great and small, that we have experienced in our lives — including having a roof over our heads and enough to eat every day. Time and again the Father thinks up ways to bring His children joy. If we would thank Him for all these things and rejoice over them, our love for Him would be set on fire.

Yet where can we find homes, even Christian ones, where people praise and glorify God with cheerful, grateful, loving hearts? Yes, repent. Turn from your ingratitude, God is saying to us. Jesus entreats us to repent of grieving the Father's heart. The Father wants to rejoice over His children, yet His heart is filled with sorrow, as we often read in His Word, "You have burdened me with your sins, you have wearied me with your iniquities" (Isaiah 43:24b).

How many Christians live to bring joy to the Father out of love for Him? How many constantly bring Him praise and thanksgiving in response to all His goodness? Yes, let us repent of our ingratitude. Is it not shameful to accept God's blessings as though they were our due without thinking of the heart of the Giver, who planned them all in love for us, and giving Him the response of love and gratitude?

Oh, we are often harder than stones! God loves us as no human being could love us. He has sacrificed more for us than any human being ever could. He not only gave His very dearest for our sake, but He let His beloved Son suffer torment and agony and die for our sake. Yet we grieve God. We do not thank Him and give Him our love.

We feel ashamed if we do not love a father or mother on earth who has dearly loved us and done so much for us, making many sacrifices for us. We feel ashamed if we continually grieve and hurt such a loving heart. Therefore, should we not blush with shame and rend our hearts when we treat our heavenly Father in this way? Instead of thanking Him for His love and sacrifice and loving Him in return, we are often so cold towards Him. And if He chastens us as every good father does, we do not lovingly trust Him, but rebel against Him. When His children respond in this way, it deeply grieves His heart.

It is as though the rocks, hills and mountains and everything else in nature would resound with the call, "Repent! Search your heart. See what you have done to your God. Turn from your ways. Repent of your indifference to God, who is Love. Repent of not trusting and loving Him with your whole heart." Yes, repent and change your attitude towards God; then the kingdom of heaven will come to you. The kingdom of heaven is there where God is loved, for He is the centre of heaven. Heaven will dawn here on earth when we sons of men repent and turn from pathways where we have been sinning against love. Let us begin to show God our love, trusting Him and dedicating our wills to Him, no matter how He may lead us.

Jesus calls us to repent, because He is yearning for us, for our love. He wants us to incline our hearts to Him. Yes, He calls to us, "Turn from your ways, turn from loving the world, yourself and other people more than Me. Mend your ways by loving Me and the Father from now on. Then We shall come to you and make Our dwelling with you. And this is heaven."

The call to repentance is God's call to salvation, for if we turn from our sinful ways, we turn home to God. The more we repent, the more we come back home to God, the more we come into communion with God and the more heaven comes into our life. Could there be anything more blessed on earth than the grace of contrition and repentance? Could there be anything that we should desire more than this blessing?

Jesus began to preach the Gospel with the message of repentance. With the word "Repent" He was beckoning to us as the Saviour, offering us His love and salvation. But behind this word we can also see the grief of God that His children have turned away from Him. He needs to call them home. This is why He calls out to them, "Turn from your ways. Turn back to Me." They are far away from Him. They no longer have the relationship to Him that children have who love and trust the Father. They have become strangers to Him. Does not a father long for his children? Does he not expect them to come home? For a father without children is not a father. And a father whose children have turned their backs on him and have gone far away is a father filled with sorrow. Just as Jesus wept over Jerusalem when He wanted to gather His children as a hen gathers her chicks, the Father's heart weeps today. He mourns over His children who do not come home, although He calls them. Yes, He still laments today, for God, the triune God, is one God, one nature and the same yesterday, today and for ever.

We should repent for the times we have not come to God, but have become over-attached to a person, to our work or to the material goods of this world. He has been waiting for us, waiting in vain, and His fatherly heart was filled with grief. When He then sought to call us home through chastenings, we rebelled against Him and His actions and again refused to come home to the Father. What else should He do with us? When He receives no response, as we read in the Book of Revelation, where His calls to repentance through the centuries reach their peak, God's just wrath will descend, for there will be no other way to call men home.

O how hard mankind makes it for their God and Creator, for their Father! But it is especially His own that make it so hard for Him, for they should know their Father in our Lord Jesus Christ better. Yet so often they continue to follow their selfish ways, although they are Christians. They seek their own honour. They seek to advance their own cause while claiming to be working for the kingdom of God. They assert their rights under the guise of contending for the truth. How blind are those who call themselves His children and still dare to cling to their idols and refuse to admit that they are committing the greatest sin, the sin of not giving Him their love.

Yes, how long must God the Father call out, "Repent!" The Father's love is so often disappointed as He waits for but one thing, for His children to come to Him with a penitent heart. For the sake of His suffering love let us harden not our hearts when we hear His voice today.

Chapter 8

Repentance, the Call for Today, the Call for the End Times

"Repent!" was the call of John the Baptist, who prepared the way for Jesus. He preached but one way to receive Jesus, the way of repentance, as it is written, "Prepare the way of the Lord, make his paths straight...the crooked shall be made straight and the rough ways shall be made smooth" (Luke 3:4f.). Only if repentance has paved the way, making the rough places smooth and removing the stones, can Jesus, the King, come. Then He will find a pathway to come to the sons of men. In other words, John the Baptist shows us that Jesus needs people to prepare the way through repentance. This is how it was at Jesus' first coming, and this is how it will be at His second coming, as Scripture tells us in many ways. It is written that before Jesus comes again in the end times Elijah will appear again as a preacher of repentance (Malachi 4:5), and that mankind will repeatedly be called to repentance, as for instance by the two witnesses (Revelation 11:3-6).

Repentance, as well as judgment, must start with the believers. Then later, at the close of the age, a tremendous movement of repentance will sweep through the people of Israel when the Messiah appears and they recognize the One whom they have pierced. But how should they repent if the Christians do not lead the way? When Jesus returns as the Bridegroom coming for His own, who is it that will be "caught up" to Him if not those living in a state of repentance? We read that long ago He first came to those who had been disciples of John the Baptist (John 1:35-42) and were in this movement of repentance. These were the first ones that He called to be His disciples. And when He comes again, it will be no different.

In our times our responsibility as individuals and as a church is doubly great, for the need to repent is more urgent than ever. We are living at the dawn of the end times, in the nuclear age and at the same time in the age when the promises for Israel are being fulfilled. The fig tree is beginning to put forth its leaves. The Jews are returning to the land of their fathers as Scripture has prophesied. In the end times heaven is waiting, the whole earth is waiting for people to repent and to prepare the way, so that the Lord can finally lead His own to consummation and take them to Himself, that at last the long wait of creation will come to an end, because the redeemed of the Lord will have come home to Zion, having been completed in number and attained full maturity.

Yes, all mankind, the whole world, is waiting for people to repent. In this terrible age, which is threatened by a nuclear war, what could be more imperative than the call "Repent"? The nuclear age has one thing to say to us: the most terrifying judgments are imminent. Do not the wars that threaten to break out, the judgments and scourges that will descend upon mankind, bear resemblance to the trumpet judgments? Revelation 8 and 9 describe how nature will be devastated and how such a war will bring death to a third of mankind. But although the Book of Revelation has been read throughout the centuries, never before could man have imagined how such things would come true. Now even a child knows that the time will soon come. The first symptoms are already with us. The damage caused to nature by nuclear tests is but an indication of what is to come.

Judgments are impending such as the earth has never seen before. In former judgments it was always God's concern that the people would repent. Thus we know that when the most terrible judgments are about to descend God will be even more concerned that people come to repentance. Yes, today this call is so powerful that it cannot be ignored, for now is the last chance to prepare for the Lord's return. In the Book of Revelation we see how great God's desire is that people repent. At every blow of judgment (whether it be during the trumpet judgments or the outpouring of the bowls of wrath), God's one question is always, "Will they repent?" But how often do we read, "They did not repent" (see Revelation 2:21; 9:20f.; 16:9,11).

Oh, that this would not be said of us! For when the judgments of God reach their peak, then it is time for the repentance of the Body of Christ to reach its peak. There should be one great movement of repentance among

Christians. How else should God save His own from the judgment of wrath? Who could otherwise escape His wrath? Truly, Holy Scripture has but one answer: those who have a contrite heart and repent. And Jesus wants His own to be spared the wrath. Scripture tells us that His own will be raptured before the terrible sufferings of the antichristian era reach their peak. This is why Jesus speaks of escaping the terrible things that will happen. In Luke 21:36 He challenges us to be awake in order "to escape all these things that will take place, and to stand before the Son of man."

Yes, we need to wake up and repent. We need to change our ways, so that we shall really be delivered out of these terrible judgments. How will that happen? If we let ourselves be judged, day by day, in our personal lives and in our churches. Only those who accept judgment in this way and love Jesus as their Judge, allowing Him to deal with every area of their lives, will be able to receive Jesus as the Bridegroom when He comes again (2 Thessalonians 1:7-10). On the other hand, we read in the Book of Revelation about those who did not want Jesus to be their Judge beforehand. When He appears to them in His mighty wrath, they cry out for the mountains and rocks to fall upon them and hide them from the wrath of the Lamb (Revelation 6:16).

The end time is a time of judgment. We have now entered this age. Therefore, it is high time to mend our ways and repent, so that we might be delivered from the judgments of wrath. That will be the grace of the rapture. Rapture means being raptured away from this world while it is undergoing judgment. It means being lifted out of the judgments and caught up to the Lord (1 Thessalonians 4:16-18). It will be only the true believers who have been cleansed from within that will take part in the rapture; without holiness no one will be able to see the Lord (Hebrews 12:14). When Jesus appears and is revealed as the Holy One of God in His majesty and divine glory, no one can enter His immediate presence or take his place beside Him if he has not been sanctified and transformed into the image of Jesus. And such can happen only along paths of chastening, when we allow Him to judge us.

Thus like a trumpet call from heaven the call to repent is sounded now in the end times. Who will take up this call and pass it on? For now it is imperative to call the Body of Christ to repentance, so that movements of repentance will arise in all nations and in all parts of the earth. Then the Lord will be able to defer and mitigate His judgments. God does not only want us to repent for our own sakes (so that we as individuals shall be delivered out of the terrible things that will come); He wants us to repent, because we are responsible for our nation and for mankind, which is heading towards terrible destruction. The time of grace, the time of God's patience, will soon be over and the wrath of God will descend upon the world. Do we have any idea how terrible the judgments of God will be when they descend upon the world? Considering the past, we may assume that our German nation will be especially struck, for our hands are stained with the blood of six million Jews. Our repentance should be in the same proportion. In the same proportion a great lamentation and weeping should break out in our midst.

But it is we, the Christians, who have been storing up God's wrath against ourselves with all our periods of impenitence. Oh, that we would not persevere in impenitence in these last times! When Jesus came to earth the first time, it was the Pharisees and many of the "pious" who did not want to be shaken out of their self-assurance. They said, "Why does John the Baptist have to be so one-sided? Why does he always have to preach repentance?" Today it is the same. If someone emphasizes repentance time and again, many think that it is fanatical, one-sided or gloomy Christianity. They say it is not the Gospel. And yet it is biblical; yet it is the Gospel, because contrition and repentance bring us forgiveness of our sins, true joy and salvation. This is the only way that Jesus can come to us, the only way that we can be delivered from judgment. This is why the message of repentance is highly relevant for our day. For abundant grace will be given to those who have a repentant heart in the end times. As the world heads for immeasurable judgment, the penitent will experience divine grace beyond compare. Jesus will come again in the clouds of heaven in magnificent glory and beauty, and He will take them to Himself. Yes, in the twinkling of an eye they will be transformed. The more they were humbled in repentance, the more they will be exalted now. Once they wore the garment of repentance, the garment of tears, weeping over their sins; now they are clad with resplendent wedding garments, shining like the sun (Matthew 13:43) as they enter into the wedding hall.

Yes, repentance and judgment should be in proportion to each other. And in proportion to the repentance will be the pardon and the glory that will follow, and they are beyond comprehension. Thus the call to repentance is God's call for the end times, and in His Word He says, "Blessed are they that hear the word of

God, and keep it" (Luke 11:28 AV and cf. Revelation 1:3; 22:7). Blessed are those who respond to this call to repentance, which is God's offer of love. They will experience a foretaste of the kingdom of heaven here and now. Nor is that all. They will be prepared for the Lord, prepared to celebrate the Marriage Feast of the Lamb with Him. "He who testifies to these things says, 'Surely I am coming soon.' Amen. Come, Lord Jesus!" (Revelation 22:20).

Prayer

Dear Lord Jesus,

I ask You for what I long to have in my life: Your great gift, contrition and repentance. Send me by Your grace the Spirit of truth, that I may see myself in Your light and know the depths of my sin. Let Your Word convict me as Your standard for my thoughts and words, for what I do and fail to do, for my work and activities. Keep me from applying my own cheap standards. Let me take as binding the standard of the Sermon on the Mount, that I may see myself as You see me, that I would judge myself as You would judge me one day if I do not repent of my sin.

Through Your Holy Spirit help me to discern Your loving admonition in everything that happens to me, especially in Your chastening. And grant me the grace to respond to it willingly.

Hear my prayer and grant me a broken and contrite heart, not one that perseveres in self-righteousness and self-complacency, but one that is able to weep over its sins and is then able to rejoice over Your forgiveness.

I thank You. You will surely answer this prayer for ever-new contrition and repentance, for there is nothing that can bring more joy to You than a sinner who repents and nothing You desire more from us than tears of repentance. I do not want to keep my eyes fixed upon my hard, impenitent heart, but I shall look to You, my Lord Jesus Christ. You came to destroy all self-righteousness and hardness of heart, and by Your redemption You have won for me a new heart that is soft and humble.

Therefore, help me to persevere in prayer and faith until my hard heart has melted and I am able to weep over the things I have done to God and to my fellow men. I know You will give me the grace to weep over my old nature, over my harshness, lack of mercy and kindness, my gossiping, my jealousy and envy, my untruthfulness, my false attachment to people and material things of this world. You will bring about a complete change in me.

I thank You, O Lord, for You will create in me what I am lacking — repentance — so that my life will be completely transformed and that out of contrition divine life and love for You will grow in my heart. Through my joyful life as a pardoned sinner, let me praise You here on earth and be prepared for Your return, so that I may celebrate with You the Marriage Feast of the Lamb in the heavenly glory.

Amen.

Other Books by the Same Author
from Bethany House Publishers

Behold His Love. A book of meditations on the sufferings of Jesus.

Father of Comfort. Short devotionals for every day of the year meant to teach the reader how to put confidence in the Father in every circumstance.

Hidden in His Hands. Devotional readings written to help the reader prepare for the uncertainties of the future.

I Found the Key to the Heart of God. The intimate life story of the founder of the world-renowned Evangelical Sisterhood of Mary. An autobiography.

Mirror of Conscience. A booklet designed to help you examine your own heart. Well suited to devotional use.

My All for Him. Meditations on how to live for Christ and thereby attain true happiness.

Praying Our Way Through Life. A booklet showing prayer as a way of life operative through daily situations.

Realities of Faith. The incredible true story of M. Basilea Schlink's ministry and the amazing miracles of faith that brought it into existence.

Ruled by the Spirit. A book that shows the inspiring power of God to guide dedicated individuals is still operative and available today.

Those Who Love Him. How to have a personal and continuing love for Christ.

You Will Never Be the Same. The author deals with sinful traits one by one, showing how we can be victorious in the battle against sin.